HERITAGE

The
VICTORIANS

Robert Hull

HODDER
Wayland

an imprint of Hodder Children's Books

Heritage

The Anglo-Saxons
The Celts in Britain
The Romans in Britain
The Tudors
The Victorians
The Vikings in Britain

Cover pictures: *The Royal Albert Hall(centre). A magic lantern(left); a jubilee brooch(top-right); a penny black(top-left).* **Title page:** *The Forth Bridge.* **This page:** *An early camera.*

Editor: Jason Hook / Liz Harman
Designer: Jean Wheeler
Cover designer: Jan Sterling

First published in 1997 by Wayland Publishers Limited

Reprinted 2000 by Hodder Wayland,
an imprint of Hodder Children's Books

© Copyright 1997 Hodder Wayland

A catalogue record for this book is available from the British Library

ISBN 0 7502 2811 3

Typeset by Jean Wheeler
Printed and bound by G. Canale & C.S.p.A., Turin, Italy

Hodder Children's Books
a division of Hodder Headline plc,
338 Euston Road, London NW1 3BH

Contents

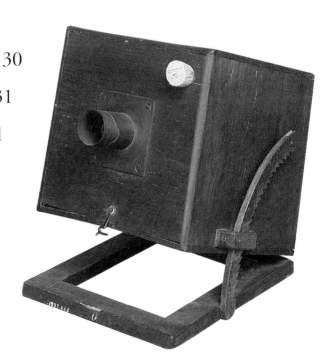

chapter one

HOW DO WE KNOW ABOUT
THE VICTORIANS?

You lick a stamp, strike a match. You open the fridge, pick up the phone. With each action, you are using a Victorian invention.

Our Victorian heritage is all around us, but the Victorian era (1837–1901) is so close to us in history that sometimes we do not notice it. The Victorians gave us railways and stations, and wonderful iron bridges like the one over the River Avon at Bristol. They gave us the family hotels along the front at Blackpool, the bandstands and promenades.

▲ *Cameras made it possible to record events like this meeting of Queen Victoria with rulers of other countries.*

Look into books to see photographs of the bandstand in action, the promenade crowded. The camera was a Victorian invention. The first Kodak camera came on the market in 1888 with the slogan: 'You press the button, we do the rest.'

▶ *One of the first cameras, made by Kodak.*

We can also learn about the Victorians from their writing, in diaries, letters and novels. The Victorians still tell us their stories. All over the world today, people read books such as *Oliver Twist, Alice in Wonderland, The Adventures of Sherlock Holmes, Treasure Island, Dr Jekyll and Mr Hyde* and *Jane Eyre.*

Victorian inventors changed our world. Scientists invented the motor car and developed electric light. They made important discoveries and created new ideas.

We can still read the naturalist Charles Darwin's fascinating description of finches and turtles on the Galapagos Islands. He observed how the different species had developed or 'evolved', an idea that changed the way we understand life on earth. The Victorians still fill our minds as well as the rest of our lives.

A writer in the 1970s could still recall his Victorian childhood: 'I can remember a Victorian tea-table at which there were always eight plates of sandwiches, cakes, biscuits and so on, whether anyone had been invited or not.'

▼ *The Clifton Suspension Bridge, designed by Victorian engineer Isambard Kingdom Brunel and completed in 1864.*

chapter two

WHO WERE
THE VICTORIANS?

Queen Victoria's reign from 1837 to 1901 was the longest in British history. The people of that time are known as the Victorians. They lived through a sixty-year period in which life changed more than ever before in history. One prime minister, Lord Salisbury, described Victoria as 'the bridge over that great interval which separates old England from new England'.

Victoria's husband, her German cousin Prince Albert, was also her private secretary. 'His laws about everything are to be my laws,' she once said. Prince Albert sometimes took Victoria's place at meetings with the Privy Council, which made important decisions about the running of the country.

▼ *A portrait of Prince Albert, who was both husband and adviser to Queen Victoria.*

In 1861, when Albert was dying, he changed the wording of an angry letter from the Foreign Minister, Viscount Palmerston, to the USA. If Albert had not done this, there might have been war between Britain and the USA. Part of our heritage is peace between the two countries.

In Victorian times, Britain was run by politicians, just as it is today. Victoria thought that she had a part to play in political life. She believed that the queen's role was important, and she often gave advice to ministers. Victoria had to sign many documents and letters, and sometimes she asked for changes. One prime minister, William Gladstone, nearly resigned because he felt that she was interfering too much.

▲ *A brooch commemorating Victoria's diamond jubilee.*

▼ *A cup made in 1897 to celebrate the diamond jubilee.*

After Albert's death in 1861, Victoria stayed out of public life for many years. She gave up opening Parliament, and spent a great deal of time at Balmoral, in Scotland. For the rest of her life she dressed in black.

Late in her reign, Victoria became a popular public figure. She made many official visits, down a Cornish iron mine, to Parkhurst Prison and into wards of London hospitals. She also took a keen interest in housing problems. Queen Victoria seems modern, but in some ways she was not. She did not like the idea of women doctors and once spoke about 'the mad, wicked folly of women's rights'.

chapter three

HOW IMPORTANT WAS THE
BRITISH EMPIRE?

The British Empire was vital to Britain's expanding industries. Companies needed to buy raw materials such as tin, rubber and copper from abroad, and they required markets around the world to sell their goods.

Britain's right to trade with a country was first established by trading companies. Later, Britain might use its military power to claim 'sovereignty' over that country. It then became a 'colony' in the British Empire. In Asia, Chinese attempts to stop British drug-traders selling opium led to war. Britain defeated China and claimed sovereignty over Hong Kong, which remained a colony from 1842 to 1997.

In India, the British East India trading company ruled over 200 million people by employing native soldiers. In 1857, these soldiers mutinied, and there were bloody massacres. The British Army ruthlessly restored order, and India was handed over to the Queen. British rule lasted until 1947.

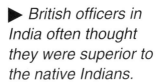

▲ *The culture of native peoples, like this New Zealand Maori, was threatened by British rule.*

▶ *British officers in India often thought they were superior to the native Indians.*

◀ *The areas marked in red were part of the British Empire during the 1800s.*

Britain claimed sovereignty over the lands of 88 million people, including Australia, New Zealand, Canada and large chunks of Africa. Islands in nearly every sea and ocean came under British 'protection'. A large part of the world that is no longer British still speaks English today.

Some colonies left a heritage of problems. Britain had to fight to keep Cyprus, in the 1950s, and the Falklands, in 1982. Ireland remains the greatest of these problems. William Gladstone, Prime Minister from 1868-74, wanted 'Home Rule' for Ireland, but the House of Lords rejected the idea. Today, many Catholics in Northern Ireland believe they should have political freedom from Britain.

In 1900, British troops were besieged at Mafeking, in South Africa, for 217 days. The commander was Robert Baden-Powell, who later founded the Boy Scouts.

▼ *The Queen in 1993, with heads of the Commonwealth, made up of countries that were once part of the British Empire.*

chapter four

HOW DID THE VICTORIANS CHANGE OUR ENVIRONMENT?

▲ *The* Derwent, *a Victorian steam train.*

A vicar wrote of one railway: 'The line will pass through only inferior property, and will destroy the abode of the powerless and the poor ... it will avoid the properties of those whose opposition is to be dreaded – the great employers of labour.'

The 1840s were the years of 'railway mania'. In 1846, there were 272 Acts of Parliament dealing with the new railways.

The first passenger railways were opened just before the start of Queen Victoria's reign. Throughout the Victorian age, brilliant engineers like Isambard Kingdom Brunel, ánd George and Robert Stephenson, continued the railway revolution. Their railway lines, tunnels, bridges, cuttings, viaducts, embankments and stations transformed the face of Britain. Many of these constructions were amazing feats of engineering, as you can still see today.

Railway building often met with angry opposition from canal owners, who knew that they would lose customers to the new form of transport. One railway surveyor described how he avoided the gamekeepers on the lands of a canal owner: 'Some men set off guns in a particular quarter ... all the gamekeepers made off in that direction [which] enabled a rapid survey to be made during their absence.'

▲ *A London to Edinburgh timetable from 1897.*

Many Victorian railway constructions are still in use. High-speed trains to Cornwall twist slowly on to Brunel's wrought-iron bridge over the River Tamar, at Saltash. They rumble over Robert Stephenson's bridge across the Tyne, which has a roadway running underneath the railway.

London's first Underground line opened in 1863, running between Paddington and Farringdon. Many roads and streets were torn up during its construction, then relaid as they appear today.

▼ *The Forth Rail Bridge, Edinburgh, was the largest in the world when it was opened in 1890.*

Changing landscapes
Much of the work of the Victorian engineers is hidden away underground. You can still walk beneath the Thames in a Victorian pedestrian tunnel. The London Hydraulic Power company used tunnels filled with water at high pressure to operate lifts and cranes, and to raise theatre curtains, well into the twentieth century. The Victorians even made attempts at building a Channel Tunnel.

▲ *The Manchester Ship Canal was carved out of the landscape in 1894.*

London's sewage is still carried by Victorian tunnels. In 1858, the River Thames was thick with sewage. During the 'great stink', paddle-steamers could hardly move for it. This problem was improved by a network of sewers and drains, designed by Sir Joseph Bazalgette. The system was finished in 1875, after thirty years' work.

The Victorians changed the landscape in other ways. They dug the Manchester Ship Canal. Deep enough for ocean-going ships, it turned Manchester into a major port. They also erected great stone dams, like the Vyrnwy Dam in Wales, which still provides Liverpool with its water.

Better sanitation was one of many changes that improved the nation's health. Town councils made space for public parks, called 'walks'. Three opened in Manchester in 1846, the first city parks outside of London. Walks like Liverpool's Stanley Park were called the 'lungs of the cities'.

These works were made possible by outstanding Victorian engineers like Brunel. At the age of twenty-one, he designed the Thames Tunnel. He planned the Great Western Railway from London to Bristol, and rail bridges like the one at Saltash, in Cornwall.

Brunel also designed the SS *Great Britain*, which was the world's first propeller-driven ocean liner built of iron. One of his later ships, the SS *Great Eastern*, was used to lay telegraph cable beneath the Atlantic – another hidden heritage of the Victorian engineers.

▲ *Brunel at the launching of the* SS *Great Eastern, in 1857.*

◄ *SS* Great Eastern, *in 1866, laying the Atlantic Telegraph Cable between Ireland and Canada.*

chapter five

WHAT VICTORIAN BUILDINGS CAN WE STILL SEE?

The Victorians liked grand buildings. Town councils competed to put up the biggest and best town halls and museums. It is not surprising that they have left us many famous public buildings, particularly in London. These include the Houses of Parliament, the Royal Albert Hall and the New Royal Opera House in Covent Garden.

▼ *The Royal Albert Hall, in London, built in memory of Prince Albert.*

It is sometimes hard to identify a Victorian building, because Victorian architects liked copying styles from other periods of history. The 'Gothic' look copied medieval architecture, using high, pointed window-arches. The former hotel at St Pancras station and many Victorian churches, hospitals and schools were built in this Gothic style.

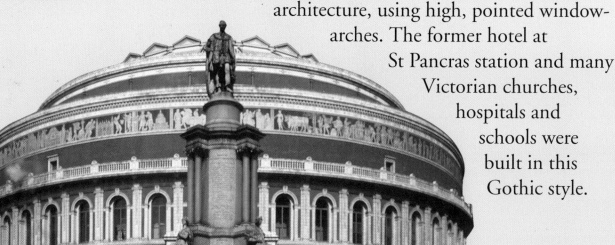

Some large houses have an 'Italian' look, while many town halls in the north of England, and many railway stations, look more 'classical', like Roman or Greek designs. The British Museum, completed in 1847, was built in this style.

Victorian gasworks are large and easy to see. So are dry docks, like those in Portsmouth and Southampton. A wander around many towns will also reveal an old waterwheel, kiln, brewery or engine house. They are reminders of the machines and factories that powered the many new industries of Victorian times.

Most factories, with their tall chimneys, have gone. But the grid pattern of streets in industrial cities remains. At Saltaire, in Yorkshire, you can still see the rows of small, back-to-back houses, built as homes for workers.

Much bigger, detached houses, for the prosperous middle classes, were built well away from factories. Today, they fill the woody suburbs of many towns. They are still desirable places to live. Signs of Victorian luxury remain visible, such as coloured tiles and stained glass.

▲ *The 'Gothic' St Pancras Station, built in 1868.*

chapter six

WHAT VICTORIAN
INVENTIONS DO WE
USE TODAY?

▼ *'Magic lanterns',*
like this one made
in 1880, led to
the invention
of cinema.

So many things that make up our modern world, and which we take for granted, seem to have been Victorian ideas. It is as if the modern world were mainly a Victorian invention.

A list of Victorian 'firsts' would make a book in itself: the first camera, the first cinema pictures, the first fridge, the first motor bus. The Victorians used matches, artificial fertilizer and even the first computer (called an 'analytic engine'). Not all these things were British inventions, but they were passed on to us by the Victorians.

In medicine, the British doctor Joseph Lister first used the 'antiseptic system'. His idea that good hygiene during operations would prevent infection has made modern surgery much safer.

The first matches came with warnings, like fireworks today. The warning printed on a box of Walker's 'friction lights' read: 'If possible, avoid inhaling the gas that escapes from the black composition.'

◀ *Two cameras used in the invention of photography by William Henry Fox Talbot in 1840.*

One of the biggest changes in the lives of Victorian people was the introduction of electric light. Early gas lamps were dim and smelly, and gave off fumes that could put you to sleep. One writer suggested that the best way to light a room was by placing the gas burner outside the window! In 1879, Joseph Swan demonstrated the first electric light bulb. Soon, the Houses of Parliament had electric light, then some hotels, ships and trains. Gradually electric lights were installed in people's homes.

An order for electric bulbs could have been made using the Victorian inventions that changed the way in which we communicate – the typewriter, the telegraph, or the telephone pioneered by Alexander Graham Bell in 1876. Orders could have been made in the same way for Mr Bowler's new hats, a Kodak camera, or a 'safety bike' with the new, inflatable tyres made in Scotland by John Dunlop.

▼ *The 'safety bicycle', introduced in 1885, had a chain, wheels of equal size, and inflatable tyres.*

Queen Victoria was among the six million people who visited the Crystal Palace in Hyde Park, in 1851, to witness the 'Great Exhibition' of over 100,000 new inventions and machines. She described, 'The tremendous crowds, the joy expressed in every face, the immensity of the building ... it was and is a day to live forever.'

▶ *A three-wheeled motor car, designed by the German Karl Benz in 1888.*

▼ *The first motor car exhibition at Tunbridge Wells, Kent, in 1895.*

Transport and Communication

When Victoria came to the throne, Britain was already in the grip of the 'Industrial Revolution'. Inventions like James Watt's rotary steam engine of 1782 had transformed industry. Goods could now be mass-produced in factories, on machines powered by steam.

The Victorians invented new ways of using steam power. They built bigger engines for pumping stations and cotton mills, for threshing machines on farms, and for fairground rides. They also invented new forms of transport, which allowed people to travel and communicate more easily.

Steam trains replaced stage-coaches. Cheap fares were fixed by law, so that ordinary people could travel widely for the first time in history. Huge, steam-powered iron ships replaced wooden sailing ships, which meant that larger cargoes could be carried more quickly across the World. In 1869, the opening of the Suez Canal, linking the Mediterranean to the Red Sea, cut the sailing time to India by half. The world suddenly seemed a much smaller place.

The first motor cars were introduced in the 1880s. At first, people thought they were just toys for the rich. Today, it is difficult to imagine the country without busy roads.

The Victorians used the new transport to start a cheap postal service. The 'penny post' was introduced in 1840, along with adhesive stamps and envelopes. Before this, mail coaches had charged for letters according to the distance they travelled. Now, a letter could be sent anywhere in Britain for one penny.

▲ *The first adhesive postage stamp, called a penny black.*

A Victorian writer said of the new mail service: 'Of all the events with which my career has been connected, no one surpasses ... the adoption of a Uniform Penny Postage ... the glory of England for all time.'

◄ *Among the letters in the penny post were Christmas cards, which were first printed in Britain in 1843.*

19

chapter seven

WHAT DO WE KNOW ABOUT
VICTORIAN LIFE?

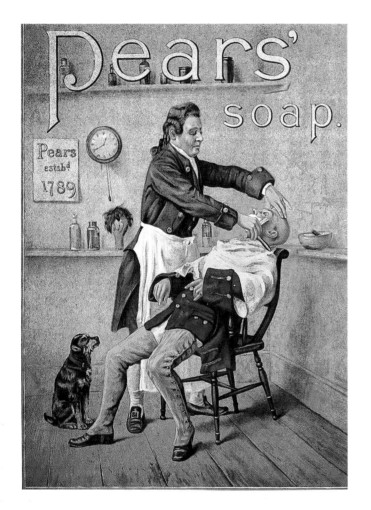

▲ *There was a growing interest in cleanliness. This advert for Pears soap appeared in 1891.*

Official reports tell us much about Victorian life. Cities grew rapidly, as workers travelled from villages to the smoking factories to find jobs. Many ended up living with their families in overcrowded slums. One report describes the homes of the poor in Birmingham as having 'bowing roofs, tottering chimneys, heaps of brick, broken windows and rough pavements, damp and sloppy'.

Many houses had no bathrooms. Families had to buy water from 'water-carts', or queue up for it at stand-pipes. In Westminster, a stand-pipe that supplied water to sixteen houses was turned on for just five minutes on Sundays – the day when most people did their washing.

Poor sanitation led to illness. In London, cholera epidemics killed thousands of people. Working conditions were also dangerous. Reports describe workers breathing in lead dust and cleaning spirits that made them 'act silly'.

A report described a bleach worker wearing 'a muzzle, composed of twenty-six folds of flannel [whose] chest heaves like that of a man struggling for breath.'

Many children had to work in terrible conditions, until Parliament called for changes. The use of 'climbing boys' – who climbed up chimneys to sweep them – was banned. An Act of 1842 prohibited children under ten from working down the mines. Fewer children went to work in factories after 1870, when it became compulsory for them to attend school. In 1891, free education was introduced.

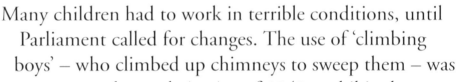

◀ *Victorian medicines. Aspirin and chloroform – which puts patients to sleep – were first used by Victorians.*

John Simon became the first medical officer for London in 1858, and called for 'a conscience against filth'. After the Public Health Act of 1872, councils began to provide clean water and sewers, and dispose of rubbish. In the hospitals, the use of a disinfectant, phenol, by Joseph Lister, reduced deaths after surgery. Army nurse Florence Nightingale returned from the Crimean War in 1856, to campaign for cleaner hospitals and proper training for nurses.

▼ *Florence Nightingale with trainee nurses in 1866.*

A divided society

The Victorian poor were very poor, the rich very rich. Flower sellers earned about sixpence a day. The Duke of Westminster took £250,000 a year just from his rents in London. More and more workers formed trade unions to seek better pay and conditions.

People became interested in women's rights in Victorian times. Victorian women were not allowed to become lawyers or join the armed forces. The few women who studied at university were not awarded degrees. When the author Charlotte Brontë married, she found that her husband was paid the royalties from her books.

Emmeline Pankhurst won wives the right to own property separate from their husbands in 1870. It was not until the twentieth century, though, that women were allowed to vote in general elections.

▲ *The seaside resort of Blackpool in Lancashire, where the famous Blackpool Tower was opened in 1894.*

Florence Nightingale once said: 'Women do not consider themselves human beings at all.'

Leisure

We inherit our idea of leisure time from the Victorians. They introduced public or 'bank' holidays, and holidays with pay for workers. They founded museums such as London's Science Museum and Natural History Museum, which we can still visit today.

After the 1850s, the railways carried the first daily newspapers, like the *Manchester Guardian,* to all corners of Britain. People could now follow national news, trends and fashions. Newspapers carried advertisements for day trips on the railways to seaside resorts like Brighton and Blackpool. Travel agents Thomas Cook offered their first railway excursion in 1841, and in 1878 they took 25,000 British visitors to the Paris Exhibition.

The Victorians enjoyed sport. They invented rules for rugby, tennis and football. The first Football League season took place in Victorian times, and the first Cup Final was in 1872. Ten years later, English cricketers first played against Australia for the trophy known as the Ashes.

▲ *An advert for one of the first cinema shows, in 1899, which included film of the FA Cup Final.*

One woman from a well-off family said: 'Even when I first married, it would never have occurred to me that I could possibly be the cook myself ... Ladies were ladies in those days; they did not do things themselves, they told other people what to do and how to do it.'

◄ *A football international between England and Scotland in 1872. England won 1–0!*

chapter eight

WHAT DO WE KNOW ABOUT VICTORIAN POLITICS?

In 1872, at a local election in Pontefract, Yorkshire, people cast their votes in secret for the first time. Before this, people were sometimes forced to vote a certain way, perhaps by their employer or landlord. Today, people are free to vote how they wish, without anybody else knowing.

▼ *The Houses of Parliament.*

During Queen Victoria's reign, more power passed to 'the people'. An act of 1884 gave the vote to all men over twenty-one, including the poorest agricultural workers who had not been allowed to vote before. The voting rights of the workers led to the increasing power of trade unions, and the founding of the Independent Labour Party in 1893.

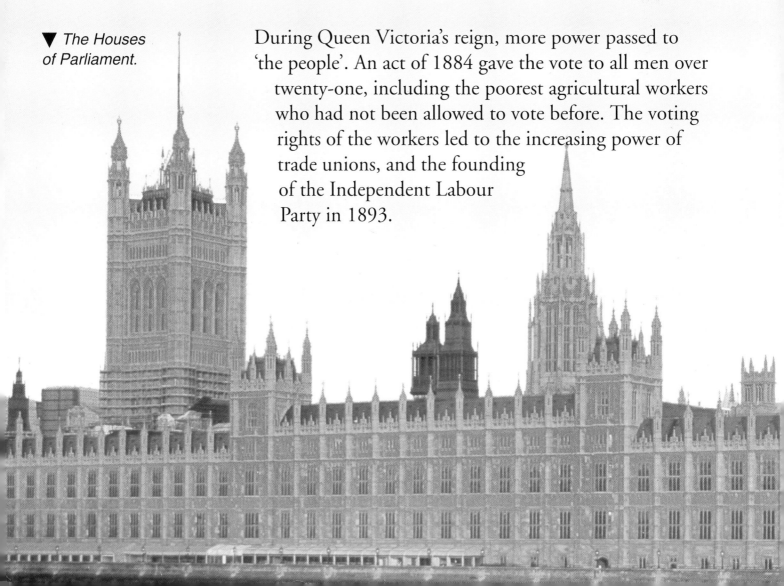

▲ *Prime Minister William Gladstone, the 'Grand Old Man' of British politics.*

William Gladstone, one of Victoria's prime ministers, began the tradition of going on the 'election trail'. He travelled by train and made speeches to huge crowds, in an attempt to win votes. Victoria also made nationwide tours. Her visit to Ireland at the age of eighty-one was captured on film.

By 1901, the Queen had become a spokesperson for the Government, rather than a political figure. The House of Commons had become stronger, the monarchy weaker.

Today, Members of Parliament (MPs) come from all walks of life. However, until an Act of Parliament in 1858, people had to possess a certain amount of property before they could become MPs.

There was also a major change in the home of British politics, after the old Houses of Parliament burnt down in 1834. The magnificent building that we see today, with its 1000 rooms and 100 staircases, was completed in 1867. At one end was the Westminster Clock Tower, in which the bell, Big Ben, has chimed the hour ever since.

chapter nine

DO VICTORIAN IDEAS STILL AFFECT US?

Every day, in the imaginations of readers all over the world, Oliver Twist asks for more, Dr Jekyll turns into Mr Hyde and Sherlock Holmes peers at a clue.

Lewis Carroll's book *Alice in Wonderland* was published in 1871. In it, the Mock Turtle tells Alice that at school he learned: 'Reeling and Writhing ... and then the different branches of Arithmetic – Ambition, Distraction, Uglification and Derision.' That same year, Edward Lear published a book of nonsense rhymes, including one you may know: 'The Owl and the Pussy Cat went to sea, in a beautiful pea-green boat ... '.

The Victorian period was a great time for poetry. William Wordsworth, Alfred Lord Tennyson, Thomas Hardy, Christina Rossetti, Elizabeth and Robert Browning were all Victorian poets.

Thomas Hood's 1843 poem *Song of the Shirt* is about people who worked for very low wages: 'Work, work, work? My labour never flags; And what are its wages? A bed of straw, A crust of bread and rags.'

▲ *An illustration from* Alice in Wonderland, *in which Alice meets the Cheshire Cat.*

Victorian paintings and novels show parts of our Victorian heritage. The early steam trains inspired Joseph Turner's famous painting of 1844, *Rain, Steam and Speed*. Holiday crowds at the races were shown in *Derby Day*, painted by William Frith in 1858.

▲ Derby Day, *a painting by the artist William Frith.*

▼ *This cartoon of Darwin makes fun of his idea that humans might have evolved from apes.*

Writers looked around them, and did not always like what they saw. In his 1854 novel *Hard Times*, Charles Dickens wrote about 'Coketown', an imaginary city polluted by factories. He describes 'tall chimneys, out of which innumerable serpents of smoke trailed ... a black canal, and a river that ran purple with evil-smelling dye.'

We still use Victorian ideas to think with. The naturalist Charles Darwin observed many different breeds of finches on the Galapagos Islands. He believed this showed that species had not been created as they now were, but had developed or 'evolved' over the centuries. The idea of evolution challenged the Bible story of the Creation, and created furious arguments. Some people today still refuse to accept it.

chapter ten

WHAT OTHER LEGACIES REMAIN FROM THE VICTORIANS?

▲ *Frames from the first successful British film,* Incident at Clovelly Cottage, *made in 1895.*

By 1901, life had changed a great deal. Motor cars had arrived. People could go to see films at 'Kinemas'. There were tinned foods in the larder and a carpet sweeper in the cupboard. Other, less obvious changes were happening. Many parents wanted their children to stay longer at school. Women wanted to vote.

There was an increasing desire to help the less fortunate. The Salvation Army was founded in 1878 to fight drunkenness and poverty. Dr Barnardo's charity looked after homeless children. Co-operative, or 'Co-Op', shops provided goods at low prices. All three organizations are still working today.

Some industrialists, such as the Fry, Cadbury and Rowntree families, worked to improve the lives of their workers. In 1895, George Cadbury built the Bourneville estate of workers' houses in Birmingham. There was plenty of land around these houses for parks and recreation. This idea led to 'garden cities' such as Welwyn Garden City being built.

One Victorian writer said about the new motor cars: 'They've come to stay. Just so much more rattling round of wheels and general stink.'

This passage written in 1892 could have been written 100 years later: 'There are hundreds and hundreds who sleep every night in the parks ... It is a sight to cross London Bridge after midnight, and to look at the recesses filled with poor homeless ones in all attitudes, trying to snatch in sleep a few hours' relief from life's misery.'

◀ *A Salvation Army shelter in 1899.*

▼ *The clock at Greenwich, by which we set our watches.*

Before the railways, clocks in different parts of Britain were set to slightly different times. For train timetables to work, the time had to be the same all over the country. So, after 1884, everyone set their clocks by the time in Greenwich, London, which is at 0° longitude on the map. This was known as Greenwich Mean Time, and we still set our watches by it today.

The Victorians were great believers in 'progress'. Perhaps, without thinking about it, our minds make use of this Victorian idea. But have we still got their confidence in 'progress'? Would they solve some of our problems more quickly than we are doing?

Glossary

GLOSSARY

Antiseptic Preventing the spread of germs.

Architects People who design buildings.

British Empire Countries across the world under British control.

Cholera An infectious disease.

Colony A settlement partly ruled by the settlers' country of origin.

Commonwealth A group of countries that were once ruled by Britain.

Conscience A moral sense of right and wrong.

Diamond jubilee A celebration of sixty years.

Dry docks Enclosures for repairing ships out of the water.

Engineers People who make machines and constructions.

Epidemics Widespread occurences of a disease.

Evolved Developed into a new form.

Folly Foolishness.

Home Rule Government of a country by its own citizens.

Industrial Revolution The rapid development of industry, particularly in Britain in the eighteenth and nineteenth centuries.

Kiln A furnace for baking clay.

Longitude The distance in degrees east or west of Greenwich.

Magic lanterns Early forms of slide projectors.

Mania Great enthusiasm, obsession.

Mass-produced Made in very large quantities, by machines.

Mutinied Turned against one's own officers.

Naturalist A scientist who studies animals or plants.

Privy Council A monarch's advisers.

Progress Improvement, move forward.

Promenades Paved seaside walks.

Royalties Money paid to an author for each copy of their book sold.

Sanitation The disposal of sewage and rubbish.

Sovereignty Power of ownership.

Stand-pipes Temporary taps extending from the water mains.

Suburbs Areas on the edge of a city.

Surveyor Someone who examines land before purchase (e.g. for railways).

Telegraph A system for sending messages by electrical signals.

Trade unions Groups of workers organized to protect their rights.

Viaducts Bridges carrying railways or roads across valleys.

BOOKS TO READ

Deary, Terry *The Vile Victorians* (Scholastic, 1994)
Deary, Terry *Who Shot Queen Victoria ?* (Watts, 1997)
Dickens, Charles *Hard Times* (Penguin, 1995)
Hicks, Peter *The Victorians* (Wayland, 1995)
Langley, Andrew *Victorian Britain* (Hamlyn, 1994)
Shuter, Jane *Victorian Britain* (Heinemann, 1992)
Wright, Rachel *Craft Topics: Victorians* (Watts, 1994)

PLACES TO VISIT

Many buildings, roads and railways near you were probably built in Victorian times. Try to find out about them. You may also like to visit the following places.

Houses of Parliament,
Westminster, London.

It may be possible for your school to organize a visit to the home of British politics.

The National Railway Museum,
York, Yorkshire. Tel: 01904 621201.

Displays range from an 1829 locomotive to Queen Victoria's railway carriage decorated in blue silk.

SS *Great Britain,*
Great Western Dock, Gasferry Road, Bristol. Tel: 0117 926 0680.

Brunel's great ship was rescued from the Falklands, and towed back to the dock where it was built. Nearby is the Clifton Suspension Bridge, which you can still cross.

Science Museum,
Exhibition Road, London SW7 2DD. Tel: 0171 938 8000

There are many exhibits showing the many advances in science made by the Victorians, including models of Brunel's ships.

INDEX

Numbers in **bold** refer to pictures.

Picture acknowledgements
The publishers would like to thank the following for permitting the reproduction of their pictures:
Mary Evans *cover*(bottom-right), 4(left), 19(top), 23(bottom), 27(bottom); Hulton Getty 10, 13(top), 18(bottom), 25(top); Impact 29(bottom); Museum of London *cover*(top-right), 7(top); Billie Love 8, 13(bottom), 17(bottom), 29(top); National Portrait Gallery 6; Norfolk Museums Service 19(bottom), 21(top); Robert Opie 4(right), 11(top), 26; Pictor 1, 5, 11(bottom), 22; Science and Society *cover*(left), 2-3, 16, 17(top), 18(top), 23(top), 28; Tony Stone *cover*(centre), 14, 15, 24-5; Tate Gallery 27(top); Topham 9, 20; Wayland Picture Library 7(bottom), 12, 21(bottom).
Map artwork on page 9 by Peter Bull Design.